the shatter between heartbeats

E. T. Vale

edited by
Amir Kapoor

For permissions, bulk orders, or rights inquiries, contact:

Open Kimono Publishing, LLC

12740 York St, STE 64

Thornton, CO 80241

info@openkimonopress.com

www.openkimonopublishing.com

––––––

Library of Congress Cataloging-in-Publication Data

Vale, E.T., 1994–, author.

The Shatter Between Heartbeats / by E.T. Vale.

Description: First edition.

Identifiers:

Hardcover ISBN: 978-1-961763-99-9

Paperback ISBN: 978-1-961763-98-2

E-book ISBN: 978-1-961763-97-5

Subjects: LCGFT: Poetry.

Classification: PS3602.R6965 A6 2025 | DDC: 811.6

LCCN record available at https://lccn.loc.gov/

––––––

Contributors

Author: E.T. Vale

Edited by Amir Kapoor

Designed by Open Kimono Publishing, LLC

Title-page and part-opener photograph copyright © 2025 by Amir Kapoor

_____

Production Details

Printed in the United States of America

First edition, 2025

Cover and interior design managed by Open Kimono Publishing, with design by Amir Kapoor.

_____

Bulk & Special Orders

Our books may be purchased in bulk for promotional, educational, or business use. For inquiries, please contact info@openkimonopress.com.

_____

Follow Open Kimono Publishing:

Website: www.openkimonopublishing.com

Facebook: www.facebook.com/openkimonopublishing

X (Formerly Twitter): www.x.com/openkimonopub

_____

Instagram: www.instagram.com/openkimonopublishing

If you or someone you know is struggling, you are not alone.

• **988 Suicide & Crisis Lifeline**: Call or text 988, or visit 988lifeline.org for 24/7, free, and confidential support.

• **Crisis Text Line**: Text HOME to 741741 for immediate assistance, 24/7.

These resources are provided for informational purposes only and are not affiliated with the author, publisher, or this book.

introduction

There is a space between certainty and collapse. A space where the mind races, the chest tightens, and the world shrinks down to a singular, unbearable moment. A dread so palpable you can taste it. The storm followed by the calm—should the monsoon ever end. It is in this space—the shatter between heartbeats—that this collection exists.

The Shatter Between Heartbeats is not just an anthology; it is an experience. It is the rapid-fire pulse of anxiety, the quiet ache of isolation, the jagged edges of a world that doesn't slow down even when you need it to. But it is also the light that filters through the cracks, the fleeting moments of joy that feel almost too delicate to hold, the fragile balance between what breaks us and what keeps us alive.

When I envisioned this anthology, I wanted it to be more than a collection of words. I wanted it to reflect what it means to exist in a mind that is both a refuge and a battlefield. The poems inside are arranged to mirror the rhythm of an anxiety attack—the slow build, the dizzying crescendo, the sharp plunge into chaos, and the uncertain aftermath. Some pages will feel like breathing room; others may tighten around you in a blanket of fire. That is intentional. That is the reality of living with a mind that doesn't always listen.

This book is not a solution, nor does it attempt to be. It is not here to fix, to soothe, or to simplify. It is here to **be**—to stand in the rupture, to acknowledge the moments we don't always have words for, to remind us that even in the most fractured spaces, we are not alone.

To those who read these words, I hope you find something here that makes you feel seen—and allows you to embrace the beautiful, chaotic wreckage of existence, with all its highs and lows, and what it truly means to be alive.

—*E.T. Vale*

one
parceled

They flood in without cause,
slosh violently between my ears.
My mind, a poisoned well—
a fishbowl tethered at the neck,
filled with the weight of drowning thoughts.
Each wave gnaws at my brain,
a relentless erosion,
as voices rise,
a French kiss of disdain.

The taste of cigarettes—
burnt, toxic, metallic—*leeches* into me.
I don't smoke,
but I do through them,
their tongues of ash and bile
forced down my throat,
their sermons delivered in silent screams.
This is only the beginning,
the prologue to the terror.

I fight to parcel out the thoughts—

before they maul us all.
Heart pounding,
perspiration, the body's first betrayal.
My vision narrows,
pupils recoil,
as the room shrinks,
and air becomes a distant memory.
I claw at my collar,
grasping for a breath that won't come.
My voice, rasped and hollow,
shares in the ineptitude
of this twisted mess to follow.

I sit at the table,
acting normal in this meeting,
as the voices hiss their commands:
Smile, tilt your head,
Nod, show that you're listening.
But I am dying in this moment,
my consciousness slipping,
a threadbare jammed beneath my fingertips,
lost in the noise.
These voices—
they are all that's left,
and the only ones I breed.

two
motive

Subtle reminders of worldly things,
possessions of what one does and doesn't have.
A mantra of happiness pushed,
propaganda of the purchased.
They fail to see beneath the skin,
to what lies behind the lying eyes.
A sickness,
a darkness envelops the room that cries.
Healthy as a heart attack—
the sickness swells deep to win,
overtaking everything, terminally within.

Carved-out holes of clay
in a walking skeleton's head—
this is the flesh body
I take with me each night to bed.
Under the guise of normalcy,
everyone sees nothing,
only what they believe
to be their own sin.
The wounds,

the disease that cuts me off at the knees
aren't visible to those who cannot see.
Another validation of my own insanity.
In this war, no one walks away unscathed.
Because they cannot be seen,
those outside the fight
will never smell the rancid rot
of the disease's might.

three
scream

In my most vulnerable state
it finds me—I unknowingly await,
it takes form as a benign suffocation,
the ultimate fate.
I cast it away,
pulling on the strength of the Holy Spirit,
but my cries are drowned;
my voice can't inherit.

The demon births itself
in the curl of the steam,
a figure of malice, the death of a dream.
Its hands like claws—
razor sharp talons, its gaze like night,
it laughs as it smothers the flickering light.

I wield the Trinity, the sacred Three,
Father, Son, and Spirit inside of me.
But my prayers fall thin,
burning sulfur in the air,
against this creature that feeds on despair.

The towel descends, the poltergeist's coil,
engulfing me in suffocating toil.
It waterboards me on the
mildew-stained shower's flower,
a silent execution in the coldest hour.

I kick, I thrash, my lungs beg to scream,
but silence engulfs ever-desperate scheme.
The tiles are grave-cold,
the drain drinks my fear,
and still, it presses, its malice near.

My voice has fled; I am bound and blind,
as water drowns the end of my mind.
The Holy Ghost weeps, retreating in shame,
and I am left knowing it knows my name.

Beneath the deluge, my strength fades away,
the demon prevails in its cruel decay.
No hero arrives, no savior appears,
just the bleeding
sound of water and unspoken tears.
It gurgles and pools in a low, spiraling strain,
a murmuring hollow drumming
that circles the drain.

So in my most vulnerable state
it found me too late,
no spirit could save me from this chosen fate.
The shower's steam swallows
the light of my plea,
I am consumed by my choices—
the death of 'me.'

four
until tomorrow

I couldn't tell you what it's like to live.
I could tell you what it's like to die;
I do it every day.

Visceral pericardium bursts
of indescribable pain,
sharper than a razor's edge,
and you are always to blame.
It's chaos incarnate,
your soul plastered on the room's
white walls,
your brain ripped out with a shotgun,
you wait for their calls.
Your vision constricts,
a tunnel where the tracks unwind,
the pain still gnaws, but it softens;
the ending arrives in kind.

What they say is true—
everything flashes in that single beat,
images familiar yet foreign,

an unbroken loop of defeat.
An ounce of calm overtakes you,
brief but swift,
a shot of Absinthe,
a fleeting reprieve before reality shifts.
And there it stands, the blue shoebill
in its patient wait,
as the last light leaves your eyes,
surrendering to fate.

Enter the finality of totality.

It's over—until tomorrow.
And tomorrow, I die again.

To understand what it means to live,
a riddle etched in sin,
it is a task I've yet to master,
as each day is withdrawn.
A heart ensnared in thorns,
a piercing, silent pawn,
pain so sharp,
it cleaves the fragile life you make.
A storm unbound,
scattering fragments of a weary soul,
forever, for them to take.
An endless maelstrom of longing—
beyond control.
The world narrows,
a passage bleak and confined,
where agony lingers,
though its sharpness declines.

Memories cascade,

a collage fractured and frayed,
familiar and distant,
their edges blurred and decayed.
A transient peace flickers,
a brief, tenuous spark,
before the weight of existence
reclaims the dark.

And then, the curtain falls—
consciousness unwinds,
a fragile surrender,
an end that time defines.

It concludes—
only to begin again with the sun's pale climb,
the cyclical demise, relentless, time after time.

five
hold on

Everything is crumbling beneath my feet.
Failure after failure—
a macabre monument
built brick by brittle brick,
each collapse a prolific feat,
an architecture of defeat.

Stop.

Quit.

Give up.

Sit back—melt into the nothingness of the
    dirt,
gnaw on the sinew of surrender,
eat the hardtack,
tooth shattering sheet iron crackers of defeat,
dry and tasteless worm castles.

My skin crawls,

fragile potential squandered, chilling my spine,
haunted by the unreliability of
    consciousness—
that traitorous architect, our flawed design.
Spinning illusions, stitching deceit
into the seams of my waking hours.

An earthquake without epicenter,
shattering in disproportionate waves,
vision blurred,
thoughts rattling like unfastened rivets
in the rusted machinery of my rotted brain.

Disdain—
an old acquaintance,
its voice scalded raw,
familiar as the rancid stench
of bleeding meat left too long.

I stand—
knees trembling under invisible weights,
stars hemorrhaging across my sightline,
this mission no more stable
than faulty nuclear fission,
splitting me atom by atom,
consciousness fraying,
threading the narrow eye
of an exit wound stitched in a final goodbye.

The voices rise—
a dissonant clamoring chatter,
some pleading retreat,
others begging for the softness
of oblivion's underfoot.

But then—
one voice, steady,
a lone howl cutting through the static,
claiming the first chair in my mind—
worn, cracked red pleather, familiar yet firm,
like the contours of my own fractured urn.

Hold on,
it murmurs benign—not loud,
but melodic, a quiet crescendo
threaded with steady breath.

So I wait,
grip tightened around nothing,
riding the frayed coattails
of something that might still be fate,
or maybe just the fragile filament
of hope—
thin, trembling, broken—
Hold on—wait.

six
thin line

Morality, a blurry thin line, a false reality,
What's right and wrong, a societal formality.
Thoughts collide in a windfall of stale air,
Sitting high on their horse,
screaming we do not compare.

That's what's wrong
with righteousness's sheer brutality,
Living in a world where this plight
is a normality.
Rules bend like reeds
in the hands of the strong,
What we call justice
is just garbled legislation, too long.

A beggar's crime—his stomach's decree,
a rich man's sin is paid off with a fee.
One taught virtue, the other taught vice,
both were born in the grip of a dice.

The preacher proclaims
that the wicked shall burn,
but who wrote the scripture?
Who chose what we learn?
The sinner was molded in fire and stone,
while saints
were raised in the light they were shown.

A child is sculpted by hands never seen,
a mirror reflecting the places they've been.
Judge not for the path they have walked,
lest you unweave
how your own soul was chalked.

The law is a ledger, cold and concise—
who set the price and who rolls the dice?
The thief and the king, their lives intertwined,
one held the power, the other confined.

Does mercy belong to the ones who decide?
Or is justice a mask that the guilty provide?
History's ink stains the hands of the crowned,
truth is a dead man, drowned time and again.

The righteous cast stones
from their towers of steel,
forgetting the chains that they do not feel.
Condemnation comes easy
when comfort is near,
But tell me—
does virtue survive
when you starve in the clear?

So ask yourself now, if fate switched its game,
would you still wear honor, or revel in shame?
Are we our choices, or simply the sum—
of the lessons we've learned
and the places we're from?

seven
intrusive thoughts

That will have to do,
enough for the many, enough for the few.
Maybe one more time?
Maybe cast away one shoe.

The car behind is following you.
This is nothing new.
This is the stranger in the back seat,
a breath on your neck, a ghost in the heat.

Insanity, my brain's glue,
binding the cracks, bleeding straight through.
Blow out, everything must go—
a revolution, a solution, of all I know.

It's at my fingertips, the power to redo,
to rewrite, to erase, to start something new.
The cold front wafting in,
the voices call me too,
a creaking howl, a tremor—a circle I pursue.

Promise to trust these thoughts,
the many and few,
promise to follow them straight into blue.
They twist, they warp, they fall apart,
a kaleidoscope of figures shrouded in black,
beating my heart.

Next time, I'll be ready.
Come and get me already.
My hands shake and my vision unsteady,
breath hitching, pulse quick, everything heavy.

I am the fear that I love for no reason.
I am the prey, I am the lesion.
Luck waits eagerly, half awake.
It's all I have to lose, my final mistake.

The walls breathe.
The air is new.
The voices are laughing—
they know what I do.
The lights flicker, the floor bends.
The ground is slipping, nothing ends.

I am running, but where do I go?
I am drowning, but there is no flow.
A dream within a dream within a lie,
I can't trust my mind, but I still comply.

These hallucinations have got a hold of you.
They curl in my chest, they tighten the noose.
A trick of the eye, a glitch in my view,
reality fractures, the pieces diffuse.

So tell me, tell me—what's real, what's not?

A ghost supplying my every lot,
a thought best forgot?
Do you trust your mind
when it lies in your ear,
when it speaks in your voice,
but thrives on your fear?

The mirror distorts, the edges misalign,
Every reflection a trick of the mind.
The war isn't won, the war never ends—
It lives in my head. It calls itself friend.

eight
the choice that was never mine

You have come to me with many faces—
friend, lover, stranger, confidant,
killer, empty spaces.
Though you always look the same.

The clothing shifts
but the shepherd—its bearer—never does.
You are the curve of a doorway
that was never there,
the weight in a stale air
that chokes me with smoke.

You speak.
I hear you.
I know the words, but your voice...
is a wound I cannot trace.
I lose it the moment I wake.
I lose it the moment I try to hold it still.

You emerge from the bones of old dreams,

dragging behind you the ruin of every word
I mistook for truth.
The acts you have assumed
are beyond his name,
beyond any name at all—
a walking ghost without origin,
a storm without sky.

I see you behind doors I have not opened,
through windows I swore were shut.
You flicker in the periphery of my breath,
disembodied hands coiled around my ribs,
tightening.

Around every corner your dead aura chases,
not with urgency, but inevitability.
I should run.
I should claw my way into the waking world,
but my feet have memorized the path to you.
The thrill of combat,
living a thin line of life and death.
A dopamine fiend,
I can't ever fully feed or face.

You contort and cajole, leading me back
to places the light has abandoned,
to rooms where my own voice
no longer knows itself.
You open drawers in my head—
I thought I had forever closed,
memories I wish to have forgotten—
though I know I will never truly shed.
The intoxication of raw fear, living through it,
alive but dead.

You feed,
draining marrow,
draining memory,
drafting new ones.
Crafting a fake desire, I perspire.
I salivate at the thought—
to just have a taste—be back in it.
I lose myself in the present—
until I am more absence than man.

I enjoy it.

I choose it.

I love it.

I hate it.

It's an inseparable part of me.
The visceral pain, sharpened to precision,
a blade with my name carved into its handle.
A mind in complete derision.
So I sit penniless destitute on this park bench.
The night swallows me whole,
I wait for the opportunity—the inevitable
     pull.

You speak.

I hear you.
But your voice is water through my fingers,
always vanishing, erasing and retracing.
Always gone before I can say,
this is you.

This is real.
It's not.
And it's all I feel.
The numbness.

Is it you I'm chasing after,
or the visage of traumas I can't unmake?
Is it your hands,
or my own,
that pull me into the dark?
Bleeding through holes in my shoulder,
in this park.
I try to touch the blood, it's just a scar.
Outside, it's healed.
Outside—it's far.

Conflicted, I sit up,
watch the lamplights stretch long,
watch the past bloom teeth,
watch my own reflection flicker—
hesitate before I say yes.

It's moot.
The answer was written before the question.
There is nothing left to address.
This is who I am.
This is who I hate.
A normal man a monster?
Decorated with medals, chained to fate.

And still,

I follow.

I wait.

nine
eightfold thread

They flood in without cause,
subtle reminders of worldly things.
In my most vulnerable state,
I couldn't tell you what it's like to live.
Everything is crumbling beneath my feet.
Morality, a blurry thin line, a false reality—
that will have to do.

You have come to me with many faces-
it's all déjà vu, an eightfold thread.
I've been here before, though it escapes me.
A place, the feeling, one I cannot forget.
Everything on black, another bet.
A spin of the wheel of fate.
Maybe I forgot to remember
to forget the silhouette.

From the south to the north,
I've lost my compass.
An empty road of asphalt,
splitting at the seams,

paved with molten tar, crushed stone-
fossils of ancient life.
Etched in societal constructs
of white and yellow lines,
Those in which we can cross,
and those that guide.
I follow this road,
paved with our money, our sweat.
They're imperfect, cracking,
trying too to forget.

Highways, unfinished thoughts, unpaid tolls,
half-formed regrets
that hum beneath the pedal.
Each press of the gas,
as much a step forward as a step back.
Each choice a fractal of the last,
each moment passing briefly past,
a flicker between real and unreal,
the blink of an eye
that never lands on certainty.
But outside my truck, if I were stranded,
The roadways would last longer.
Their surroundings engulfing me
in their vast spread.

I was warned of the weight of the road,
the unbearable gravity of knowing,
of seeing the pattern and failing to unsee it.
The symmetry of disaster,
racing past me at eighty miles an hour—
death faster.
The rear-view mirrored edges of chaos
curling inward,

turning consequence into recurrence,
the unseen master.
How many times have I driven this road?
How many times have I mistaken its path,
for my arbitrary destination?

I reach for the wheel but my hand slips,
not through fingers, but through thought,
tires fraying
like leathered rope with each repetition,
each rotation splitting into eight, into infinity.
And if I press forward—
do I unravel, or do I steer left?

The night does not answer.
My labored breath refuses to hold still.
And the moon, in all its knowing,
watches without a word.
Vacant but present like a plant on a
     windowsill.
Swallow.
Another pill, without a high or thrill.

Somewhere, someone I once was
is driving on the other side of the road,
searching for me from behind the iron curtain,
reaching for a face that never settles,
a voice that never lands.
Questions that are answers
with loaded demands.

The dice roll, the wheel turns,
the bet is placed, the fate is sealed—
but the ending never comes.

And so I drive.

And so I chase.

And so I lose myself again, a concrete disgrace.

This is it, an eightfold thread—
the roundabout we can never truly erase.

ten
left

I love you, and I'm sorry.

I left.

It was never my intention to leave you bereft.
I can't bear another day slaving away
in this office quarry.

Please don't look for me—
you will never find me.
I am gone, but I'm not missing.
I'm done dreaming memories
that don't exist,
reminiscing.

I've gone to a place
where none of this can bind me.
I'm going to fulfill my true purpose—
just to be.
No more ruthless commands,
no more insisting.

I've wasted too many of my days wishing.

I'll admit it: I failed. It has beat me.
I let you down—quitting is my destiny.
This is real, I'm no longer resisting.
I'm done here, I'm no longer listening.

Just know that it's not your fault—it's mine.
I love you—
but I'm selfish and I'm running out of time.

Sell the house.
Throw away my things.
Do not keep a single picture,
don't think of me and forget my name.

Let the dust take my essence,
let the rain claim the roof,
let the walls forget my stories
let the absence of my silence
feast on the rooms.

Tell them I never was.
Tell them I never mattered.
Say I was a visage of solidarity, a waste of space,
a nameless lipstick stain on a dirty glass
that time has shattered.

No graves, no goodbyes, no stories.
Burn my books, let the ink melt like I have.
Eat my letters, like the birds of the feathers.
A nonsensical phrase,
that feels like it should mean something—
but its meaning remains just out of reach.

That is my life—
that is the ghost that haunts me,
it will never cease.

Let the fire consume
every word I have ever spoken,
let the smoke carry away
what I could never say.

I am not coming back.
I'm a coward.
Milk left out—rotten, pungent, soured.

I will not write. I will not call.
I left my phone. I left it all.
All I have is my watch,
the glue ticking against
my wrist, holding my bones with a clasped fist.

I want to be nothing.
I want to no longer be downtrodden.
I want to disappear so completely
that even God has forgotten.
I think He already has.
You should too.
Don't hold onto me.
Start fresh.
Let yourself live true, the life I never knew.

I'm sorry.

I love you... not that it ever mattered.

eleven
blood, sand, and bleach

My ears still ring.
Tinnitus, they call it.

But names mean nothing
when sound is eternal.
A frequency of violence,
static between my bones.

I can still smell it.
The blood, the sand, the bleach congealed—
pasted inside my nostrils, suffocating.
They scrubbed the floors, but not our lungs.

The fear still turns my stomach.
Vomit, every bodily fluid.
A purge of what I've seen.
It makes me sick—
not just the memory,
but the rigid sterility of it all.
The failed attempt to cover it.
To clean it.

It doesn't go away.

It sits, malignant inside me.
Not just static, but spreading.
A tumor of recollection,
metastasizing in silence.
I feel it swelling larger,
pushing against my ribs,
a living, breathing relic
of a place I can never un-live.

I stare at blank screens in an office scape.
An unknown cough jolts me,
skipping my heart; too much to take.
A shot of adrenaline—no gun, but still a
      bullet.
It rips me apart.

I try to quiet my mind, to eat the memories,
to swallow the past like bitter glass—
but still, they find me.
My soul is a dark hole
that consumes and combines.

I'm nauseous.
Overly cautious.
I float between timelines
reliving them again and again.
I taste blood in my mouth,
the gunpowder of sin.
A coppery tinge
sucked in through my nostrils.

It lingers.

The taste. The smell.
Blood, sand, and bleach.

A wet, molding stench
that sticks to my clothes,
that seeps into my pores,
that stains my being.

No amount of repenting
can make my soul clean.
No deep breathing
or classical music can erase it.
I am lying to myself—I can still taste it.
I am trying to live an illusion that isn't there.

Humanity in war?
Mixing the two unearths a
festering, rotting sore.
There is no humanity.
There is only insanity.
Gutting, bleeding calamity.

Blood, sand, and bleach.
Just try to un-live my reality.

twelve
precocious

Berated, deflated, unsatisfied—fated.

I hate myself.

This letter is post-dated.
I'm beyond it all, frustrated.
I stare at nothing, my eyes think.
I haven't slept, not even a wink.

I talk and no words sprout out.
I scream—no sound, no shout.
Glazed over and rolled sober, I stare.
These hands—not mine—they don't
    compare.

I have nothing left.
I've tossed everything over; life's theft.
There's nothing here.
There's nothing there.

Numbed sciatica—invicta fracta.

My mind claws at itself in the attic.
Sweating, trying to push past the physical
    static.

WE'RE GOOD—
IS EVERYBODY ALRIGHT?

I'm talking to myself alone
but not alone in the dead of night.
The terror. The repeated images.

Muzzle flashes paint my eyes;
solidarity vanishes.
Marbled, cold and dead.
It all steeps in decay—
everything in my head.
So damn close—
so damn far away.

I pack the wound with pills and words unsaid.

YOU'RE NOT GOING TO DIE!

YOU'RE NOT GOING TO DIE!

YOU'RE NOT GOING TO DIE!

The walls breathe, inhale, exhale-
all at a faster pace than I can lie.
I taste color, static visions pale.

Crawling in my skin, but my skin is melting,
blistering, grotesquely frail.

I blink, it blinks, but time keeps pelting.

FLOORBOARDS SCREAM.

DO YOU HEAR IT?

DO YOU FEEL US SMELTING?

I am the shadow behind the voice, the spirit.
I am the ghost of a body still walking,
I am the silence, the deafness, still talking.

It's FINE. It's GOOD.

It's LAUGHTER.

Splitting, ripping, seconds shatter.
I tear the door—its very hinges my charade.

Nauseous, my dry mouth sweats.
Hesitantly evolves to vomit.
The bile lingers in my throat,
no thanks to my LINX grommet.

The air is thick—synthetic formaldehyde
      suede.
Flesh feels plastic, the air is fake,
I drink the world, water drowns me- overtake-

TEETH IN MY MIND, CLENCHING.

FINGERS ON MY SKULL,
WRENCHING.

I AM NOT I, I AM NOT HERE,

I AM A MIRROR
WITH NOTHING TO REVEAL.

This is what it is, smell it,
eat it—the palpable fear.
I lose control of my bladder.
Lights overtake my eyes,
the darkness envelops the clatter.

WHAT'S WRONG?

And then—
nothing.

Empty.

You are going to die—
just not tonight.
What an un-reassuring
resolution to my solution.

I soil my pants.

Life living death.
It's a disgusting romance.
To hear the truth,
see the lies covered in clothes.
There is no hiding the inevitable.
The uncomfortable *throes*.

I've lost it.

I stare at it.

It stares back.

Sanity is insane,
it's draped in an ethereal adrenaline.
Dimethyltryptamine;
the devil smiles: I'm back.

I look up, "Hello, how are you?"
I push a smile, "Good, and you?"

thirteen
devotion

Nothing has ever been real until now.
I can't just run,
I have to maul through somehow.
We will figure it out.
I know we won't, I have every doubt.

Marvel at the devotion to a life of false notion.
Under a bridge, cooking,
injecting a toxic potion.
You can stop me from being.
Yes I can stop you from fleeing.

The mirror keeps
coughing up blood in my name,
every glance a confession, a trial I face.
The tiles are creaking
crimes through the grout,
the walls lean in, and I can't get out.

My name is a furnace, each syllable burns.
I pray to a silence that never returns.

The sky has no ceiling, no mercy, no balm—
only the scream of a dream without calm.

I scratch at the inside of skin with regret,
digging through fat and muscle
for a name I forget.
The air is too thick—it congeals in my throat,
like the noose of a sentence a traitor once
    wrote.
I've swallowed each clock hand,
I tick as I choke,
the minutes are gallows,
the hours death spoke.

There's no door, just a painting of one,
hung by the child I used to shun.
My conscience limps through the hall,
"You wanted escape?
Then build your own wall."
So I stacked every failure, brick by brick,
mortared in shame until the cement was thick.

And now I am sealed in a mausoleum mind,
clawing through choices I thought were mine.
The ceiling collapses in careful degrees,
suffocation by slow-moving memories.

Once, I believed I could exit through fire—
that pain was a furnace, not funeral pyre.
But the smoke only taught me
to stay in my place,
to drink from the ash and forget my own face.

There are no exits, just replicas drawn

on the backs of my eyelids,
dusk till dawn.
I dream of a door,
but it's locked from the floor,
and the key is made of original sin.
Slippery and sour, a pungent brass flower.

So I worship the flame that devours my lungs,
chanting in curses and coughing in tongues.
I am the engine, the piston, the heat—
combustion of self in a looped heartbeat.

An animal in the flesh with no curtain to bow,
nothing has ever been real until now.

We will figure it out.
I know we won't. I have every doubt.
Marvel at the devotion—how deeply I lie
to stay barely alive while forgetting to die.

You can stop me from being.
Yes, I can stop you from fleeing.
But neither of us ever leaves.
We just burn in our seats,
swearing we're driving,
as the car stays in park,
the fire keeps thriving.

Nothing has ever been real until now.

My devotion—
a fevered machine with no notion
of mercy, or finish, or rest.
I married the smoke in my chest.

I carry the match in my jaw,
strike it each time I speak of the law
of escape—knowing well it's a lie.
The engine howls crackling lullabies
to bones that refuse to decay,
to hunger that won't look away.

I am loyal to ruin, to rust,
to the skin turning blister, then dust.
I am loyal to almost, to might,
to pretending that morning means light.

I'll sit here forever in flame,
never moving, just mouthing a name
that was mine before time split in half.
You laugh. I laugh. But nothing can laugh.

Nothing has ever been real until now.

My devotion
is the vow
no one should ever speak—
a promise to the weak
that the cage is enough.
That the scorch is love.
That it's noble to choke
on the breath you never took.

That it's brave to stay broken.
That it's holy to cook
your soul in silence
and call it hope.
That if you suffer just right,
you'll learn how to cope.

But you won't.
You'll just burn.
You'll just sit.
You'll just swear
that this pit
isn't hell.
It's a prayer.
It's devotion.

And it's mine.

fourteen
its in the leaves

It's in the leaves,
every answer, everything that leaves.
Legs crossed, arms wired,
a crucifixion of self, wrists spired.

Coins don't clink, they hiss like steam,
pressed into pulp of a paper dream.
Green bleeds green in the belly of need,
roots choke the dirt, too hungry to feed.

I pressed my ear to the soil for a sign—
heard the market moan through the grapevine.
Leaves don't lie, but they do go quiet,
when you beg for more
in a world on a moral diet.

My mouth is a purse turned inside out,
tongue dry with the taste of soured pennies,
corrosive and hired.
I tried to pawn my breath for bread,
but breath has no value once it's said.

Branches creep and crack
in the language of loans,
interest compounding in marrow and bones.
Even autumn is taxed for its color,
a red so rich it dies duller.

I tried to grow dollars from apology,
watered guilt with ideology,
but the wind shook the bills from the bough
and laughed at my prayers: not now, not now.

The tree was always an altar of debt,
leaves pressed flat with ancestral sweat.
I traded my youth for a pocket of change,
but age came quick with a face dead,
estranged.

It's in the leaves—how they fall with grace,
as if they don't beg for a warmer place.
They let go without an ask or a scream.
I hoard each one, call it a dream.

Sleep never comes.
Only invoices and thumbs
pressing down on my chest like rent.
Every moment is already spent.

I sold my name to buy some peace.
The receipt is long and will not crease.
I folded it into a paper star,
lit it on fire,
wished from the far side of the bar.

But wishes don't bloom,

they just accost the cost.
And every cent counts what I lost.
I am the fruit that never grew—
a cost of living I never knew.

It's in the leaves,
where silence believes.
Where longing rots in photosynthetic light.
Where even the sun can't make it right.

Still I gather them.
Still I try.
Still I plant these lies in the fire.
Still I pray,
knee-deep in greed—
a garden of want,
but no soul to feed.

fifteen
the courtyard that won't wait

Staring at the wall I wait.
I want to be asleep, away from this fate.
To not be conscious—what utter bliss.

To know I have to do this again tomorrow,
face the abyss.
My eyes water, my body hesitates.
Another sleeping pill, my soul awaits.

The screaming.
It's the highlight of dreaming.
The pain, the smell of urine,
QuikClot, and blood—
the way the smoke clings
to my skin and gritted teeth.

I relive it all every night.
The nightmares, the sweating,
bleeding out, out of sight.
It's unimaginable—dying and dying again.

It's a tortuous reality—
still much better
than how tomorrow will begin.

Because tomorrow wears a name tag
and offers me coffee.

It says "Good morning"
with breath that reeks of policy.
It asks how I'm doing while eyeing my scars
and when I don't answer,
it writes me up for not smiling hard.

I'd rather be trapped in that gas-lit room,
that flash-lit tomb,
where the floor melts into limbs
and the walls splinter out
from each bullet's turn.
I never wanted this, to live, to learn.
Where fingers claw at my chest,
like they're trying to dig out proof
that I was ever something before this.

Where a voice that isn't mine
keeps begging me to sign.
Where the mirror won't stop watching.
Where I scream with no sound
and wake up chewing air like it's glass,
feeling the blood in my mouth
and wondering if this time,
maybe I bit through.

They tell me healing is a process.

I say so is torture.
And only one of them knows
how to be consistent,
the exit wound through and through.
You call it trauma.
I call it a memory
of a memory with too many teeth.
And still I choose it—every night I choose it.

The moment my head touches the pillow,
I crawl back into the fire.
My throat coated in a malignant cloud,
the smoke's bellow.

Because at least there,
I know who the enemy is.
At least there,
my pain isn't a living hell.
It's all for a reason,
at least from what I can tell.

At least there, while I'm bleeding out,
my blood keeps me warm.
Until it's mostly gone,
pooled in spiderwebs
that trickle out in an ungodly form.

Then it's cold.
Then it's black.
Then there's nothing.
Like I'm asleep, but before this last attack.

You think I'm broken.

I think I'm awake.
This is not survival.
This is not a put and take.
This is what's left of living,
and it's more than I can take.

So don't tell me it gets better.
Don't tell me you know what it's like.
Don't look at me,
Don't tell me to follow the light.

Tell me why I still set my alarm
six different times.
Tell me why I'm still here
and they're not.

You can't tell me anything; you have no idea—
and those who do, you forgot.

Staring at the wall I wait.
Tomorrow is what I'm scared of.
Tomorrow, date after date.
Knowing that there's nothing,
nothing to debate.
I'm waiting in a line
with it all on my shoulders.
I hope you never know, begging fate.
Making promises to God,
in a courtyard that won't wait.

Past that gate, home isn't home anymore.
Nothing past my front door.
I want to be asleep, away from this fate.

Tomorrow I'll go to work,
awake and never late.
I have too much,
the weight is cracking
my chestplate.

sixteen
water

I ask myself why I did it.

Water.

The path of least resistance.
A war inside, gnawing through the armistice.
A prisoner in my own body.
Mourning my life,
memories are shoddy.

I ask myself why I did it.

I did it because it was easy.
Now it eats me alive.
I mistook silence for peace,
emptiness for freedom,
numbness for healing.

I remember the day I stopped being a person.
It didn't scream.
It didn't cry.

It just folded its arms and left the jug dry.
I watched.
Not in horror or glee.

I just poured, waiting for answers.
Calmly taking my own drink.

I made choices
like slitting paper with wet fingers—
no precision, just pulp and red.
I buried apologies
in people who didn't deserve tombstones,
called my damage "a phase,"
called their pain "collateral,"
and named it survival.

A strange remnant of a man,
dead—but in denial.
I told myself it was for change, for better.
But the truth? I liked the putrescence.
It hollowed me out. That water was the barter.

It made a monster,
monsters don't exist.
Only righteous ideas,
that turn people into pink mist.

Strapped down in a chair.
If they didn't hate me before,
now hate is all they have, their only care.

Water.

It nurtured me without questions,

leveled my mind's suggestions.

Water doesn't argue.
It just takes you where gravity points.
And gravity always points down.
Six feet deep in the earth's fodder—drown.

It embraced me.
I looked in the mirror—
but I never faced me.
I made myself sick.

I ate the apple,
the forbidden fruit, the devil's trick.
Crisp. Sweet.
I drowned in deceit.
The lie of water.
A necessity to life.
A drowning alma mater.

I loved in the only way I could.
God, I loved—
but I faked it.
I feel nothing.
Only wasted.
I broke people.
Sometimes on purpose.
Mostly by mistake.
A bloodied lip, I still taste it.

Benign objects
morphed into elements of torture.
The allure of truth, *righteousness' courter*.
Duty became blood currency.

My life's work, whatever they needed it to be.
I lied, and labeled myself a secretary.

I see their faces now.
Flickers.
Flashbulbs.
Crying eyes mimicking mine
in every reflective surface.
Scrying.
Sometimes I see the white mist.
Sometimes I scream—trying.

But mostly—
I turn the light off and sit in the dark,
because I deserve the night I missed.
I sit, strap myself to that chair
and boil the memories away,
redacting my mind's lists.

I ask myself why I did it.

And the worst part is:
There is no answer.

Only water.

Waterboarding them—
but really, I was the sheep.
I was the slaughter.

And I am drowning in a life
they said I chose.

So it goes.

I didn't understand—
just a drone eating the command.

The towel is over my face.
One five-gallon jug
after the other.

Water.

One

breathless

decision

at

a

time.

Did I make a difference?

Did the water?

seventeen
the lamplighter

With consistency and quiet at dusk,
I light them all, a pointless busk.
The pole is light at the beginning of the night,
by dawn its weight blunders my lust; ignite.

I'm an afterthought.
A limited disguise you forgot.
Honestly empty, even bearing this flame.
Damn my life. Damn this deadly game.

Each step fizzles out my soul,
I wear no name. I own no past, an empty hole.
Even my eyes have learned to skip past,
escaping reflections of what never lasts.

My hands, they tremble and twitch,
my bones itch,
trying to escape my blood's high pitch.
Gripping the staff is
grabbing a knife by the blade,
it cuts me in half, shade by shade.

Who was I when the streets were dark?
Before the gas hissed out my spark?
A man? A son? A lover? A priest?
Now I'm nothing, just deceased.

What I hate the most,
the reflection in the lanterns, the ghost.
I light it. I light it. I never forget.
There's no escaping, no reset.

I'm burning alive
while they all rest their heads.
I walk in circles, tearing myself to shreds.
The creatures of the night, evil smiles, delights.
I'm immune to every effort of their frights.

This is what dying looks like slow:
you're still on fire,
but there's no glow.
You move because movement
is all that remains.
You smile because screaming
would rupture your veins.

But if God ever walks this route tonight,
let Him trip on my lamp
and swallow the light.
Let Him fall in the gutter
and ask me my name outright.
I'll give Him the silence
that he taught me in spite.

The street owns me. The world erased me.
I'm what's left when love can't face me.
So here I go—lamp to lamp.
Not a saint.
Just a faceless soldier without a camp.

A pole and a purpose that's nothing but pain.
Every idle hour until dawn, I walk, insane.
Lighting each lantern,
expecting a different spark.
Tonight I'll lay myself down
in the fountain of the park.

The water totals just an inch.
I'll lie on the pence of everyone's wish.
I have no wish, no desire.
I will carry this forever, long after I expire.

My curse: ignite, ignite.

eighteen
parasympathetic

It comes in waves.
The way they crest and crash...
It's a manifestation of my reality, the past.
Faces. Lit up by tracers.
Rounds that eat ravenously,
unbelievably savage.
The shaking, the ear-shattering bursts,
my smile:
war's spoil wrapped sparsely in recoil.

Kill or be killed.
That was the reality.
You can't escape that.
Humanity is nothing but a formal triviality.
After the fight, nothing was left.
A high,
a dwindling adrenaline rush testing sanity.

You chase it.
You're scared beyond belief,
in that very moment,
that pull is the only relief.
Then suddenly: repatriation.
That facilitation
of a bullshit attempt at reintegration.
Wear stupid clothes, show up every day.
Physically you're there, but in your mind:
a million miles away.

The nightmares.
Reliving it all, the scalding burns.
The determination
to answer an unspoken call.
I stare blankly at my computer.
None of this matters,
but still it chips away at my mind,
the key clatters.

I didn't realize the party had already started.
A black tie event, awarded.
I'm there without realizing it.
I hate these parties.
Pretending to be something parting.
Two pills and a few pulls of the bottle.
It's already starting.

The clawing at the back of my neck.
Gasping for breath,
reaching for what's gone, long left.
Shattered, I'm a wreck.
Seeing doubles, wasting away bereft.

They're gone.
But it's me that's dead.
My war had ended they said,
 not in fire, but kinetic—
I breathe, slow... parasympathetic.

nineteen
do i?

How can I be here, but there?

Everything will be okay in the end.
The lie you tell someone at their end.

It's crawling up the stairs.
It's the unbearable weight.
It's the pit in your stomach when you fall.

I'm in over my head.
I can't just walk away from this.
I'm hurling toward this ending.

We did nothing wrong—okay?

Words of false encouragement.
Truth eating itself away.
What do I believe?
Does it matter?

Narratives we sell ourselves,

to subsist *amid this shatter.*
A soft tone.
Sound of a door opening.
Is everything alright?
Do you mind sitting down?

I take a seat.
I asked myself to.
"Do you mind if we have a minute—alone?"

I try to step outside.
Waiting for the right time.
I can't get away—

Why do I keep trying?

What did he say to you?
He was checking up on me—
making sure I'm okay.

It doesn't change what happened.

Okay, we'll fix it.
Stop helping.
You make everything worse.

Then what do I do?
Everything's out of my control.
Sweat starts to bleed down my spine.
Stomach turning, heart skipping beats.

What's wrong?
Ask, but I can't tell you.
Our time is up.

How can I be here, but there?

It's carrying me.
I was hoping you would be here.
I wanted to see you.
I just want you to know.
We don't get to choose.
It's in our DNA.

One of these days—
he's going to see you,
for what you are.

We all do.

Do I?

twenty
considering

It all started the same way
it ended—
with something I could
never do.

I gave you my life,
but I still couldn't
save you.

We ran through the smoke,
a vow in our teeth,
clutching at gods
we no longer believed.

Your hands, still burning,
were colder than steel—
the blood on my skin
was the proof I could feel.

I screamed your name
into canvas and bone,

but bullets write louder
than prayers ever moan.

I stitched up your wounds
with the threads of my breath,
and still you collapsed
in the arms of your death.

You laughed when you fell,
said the sky was a door,
and stumbled right through
like you'd practiced before.

I caught at your sleeve
as you slipped out of view,
missing half your head,
I tried to put you back
together in my arms,
your death, something
that I never quite knew.

The world kept on spinning
with none of it right,
the silence more brutal
than any last fight.

You vanished so easily,
like mist at first light—
too stubborn for mercy,
too proud for the night.

And me? I'm still here,
but really I'm not.
I'm there with you,

that day we both
died. I'm unglued.

I lost everything,
my brother,
my best friend.
Anything I ever
thought mattered
fizzled out in the sand,
with you.

Considering it all,
it's grabbing at air.
Chasing adrenaline,
facing death.
Considering it all,
my world ended,
a spray of fire,
bullets slipped
past your vest.

It all started the same way
it ended—
with something I could
never do.

I wish it were me
instead of you.

It's seared into
my eyes.
The last vision
of you.

It all was fated, the way
it ended—
saving you—
something I could
never do.

twenty-one
delirium

I woke with my mouth full
of bloodless screams—
it opened, expelled a low, resonant
guttural croaking, vibrating violently.
I'm sewn to a casket buried alive.
Eyes open, but the dark had teeth.
I kick, punch—no strength
for my limbs to mobilize.
It chewed through time.
It wore my uniform.
Ripped in half the webbing of my toes.

The ceiling cracked, raining blistering plaster.
I counted every scalding burn for years.
My hands were not my hands.
My breath was not near.

There was something—
no, someone—inside the wall.
It had the shape of a man.
The silence, a bloodthirsty caw.

It waited for the fall.

Not sleep. Not waking.
My soul, my essence,
laid out for the taking.
A war between the two.
Each blink a surrender.
Each second, unmaking.
It took me there.
Back to the fire.

I was pinned beneath nothing,
and the air was the weight.
Its fingers smelled like gunpowder.
Its breath hummed a heavy lead, my fate.
Green lasers tattooed behind my eyelids—
targets taking rounds but ceasing to quake.

The figures convulsed.
I tried to shake.
They spoke in my voice.
They said, "You begged for this."
They said, "You called it choice."

I remembered the field.
But the field was my chest.
And the sky was a trigger
pressed against rest.

I saw the child I was,
saluting the flame.
He had medals for memories.
He forgot his own name.
A gaunt celebration

of violence
under the guise of protecting
terrain.

I became static,
a channel between.
God didn't answer.
God fed the bullets—
in never-ending belts obscene.
Consumed again
by the war machine.

I think I died.
Or I watched it occur—
the moment I cleaved
from the person I was.
Faulty, burning, bereaved.
Existing on the precipice of death.
None of it mattered.

I watched myself from above,
under a bomb-lit sky—
the soul of the explosion,
the thuds in my chest.
I watched myself with empty eyes
hold down the trigger
and forget the rest.
The fear, the adrenaline,
robes in the dirt,
blood pooling—feeding the
desert.

Now I sleep with the lights.
But the dark still arrives.

That same bullet
slips into my back,
just left of my spine.
It reroutes all the wires.
But there are no nerve endings left.
They say it was panic.
A synapse misfired.
But I know the truth:
I'm no longer required.
The numbness, still tingling—

I am the phantom pain.
Residual.
Less than before.
I will never be the same.
Wake me up, but I can't pretend.
I look in my eyes like they did—
and I meet my end.

Obligatory reminders:
the cycle repeats.
The dead rest—
I exist in purgatory,
forever in-between.

twenty-two
i inhaled the
house fire

I didn't lose my anger.
It fled.
After chewing through the leash
and dragging me,
caving in my head.

No—
that's too neat.

Let me start again.

I taught my anger to wear a necktie.
To stand in fluorescent rooms
and make budget suggestions
while clenching a jaw full of blood.

I disguised it
as productivity.
Turned it into a résumé.
Called it resilience
while it tore out the drywall inside me

just to press my
fingernails into
the nails
protruding from the studs.

There were years I ruled it—
years it stood in the corner
like a punished god,
waiting.
I was peace.
I was wrath.
I had the switch,
to control it en masse.

Until one Tuesday,
at 16:42,
a door slammed.
I fell to the floor.
Ripped the confinement
of my cubicle in two.
Someone laughed
at the wrong volume,
and the god stood up.

I felt the rage.
I didn't have control.
I felt the absence of architecture.
Every hallway in me relapsed.
Every "I'm fine" caught fire.

My mouth didn't move—
just tunnel vision,
shaking as my heart
collapsed into

a venom adrenaline flood.
Watching the beast
perspire.
But the room caught something feral
in my stare—
the kind of silence
that knows how to gut a deer,
erase innocent life
without a glance
or thought,
no care.

I dug into the
coffin of my bag.
Fumbling for the
pill bottle in a
sea of medications,
my fingers found the
plastic drag.

A pill.
No thrill,
no relief.
Just the knot
of the necktie.
It ties it neatly,
before the chair
is kicked out from
beneath me.
Hanging on fleece.

They asked if I needed a break.
I couldn't answer.
I was relearning how to breathe

without setting off alarms.
I left.
There was nothing else I
could do,
my head
trapped away so far.

Tell me again
why we can't
hold down a job—
as if the fire
should apply
for clerical work.

I've since been told
my anger is disproportionate.
As if I wasn't built
from all the hands that hit me.
As if I chose
to become this matchstick cathedral.

No one sees the altar.
The hymns written in teeth.
The pews carved from restraint.

They just smell smoke.

I miss the version of me
who could command it—
who could sip the fire
without swallowing the ash.
Who turned every insult into fuel
and every betrayal
into a brighter burn.

But now,
I am the pile of
accelerant-soaked rags.
The smoldering insulation.
The part of the house
that never stops coughing.

And when they ask
what I do for work,
I tell them:

"Containment."

But what I mean is—
I am the fire I failed to control.
And the forest
has already named me
god.

twenty-three
the call that never came

I waited.
In the dark,
sweating through the seams
of my second skin—
that uniform you kissed once
and never again.

I waited.
For orders.
For meaning.
For the voice that turned
kill
into purpose.

I waited.

And you
never
came.

Not the flag.
Not the trumpet.
Not the goddamn hand
on my shoulder,
two squeezes—
we move forward.

Just a checklist.
Just a half-empty room.
Just the echo of her heels
in your hallway,
and a door that wouldn't
even click shut.

You didn't let me go.
You let me
live just to die.

You broke my bones
by not saying my name.

That's the thing no one tells you—
it's not the bullet.
It's the silence after the bang.
The stillness
that gnaws.

I carried your war in my womb
until it turned septic.

You think it's metaphor?
Ask my insides.
Ask the blood seeped in my mattress
stitches frayed, falling apart.

I loved you
more than I loved
myself.

And I enlisted
for both.

I would've died for you.
But instead—
I lived.

Which is worse.

Every morning,
I survive the aftermath
of your indifference.

I fold the flag
of your body
in my chest
and beg,
"Recall me."

A request always
denied.

Do you know what it means
to give someone
your whole
and get back
nothing
that bleeds?

They said,
"Thank you for your service."
But not you.

You said,
"Make sure the keycard's turned in
before noon."

An unceremonious discharge.
A vanishing act.

You ghosted me
with full honors.

I dream in static.
TV snow
on motel ceilings.
The smell of cordite
and burnt sugar
from the last letter
I never sent.

I mouth your name
like a field dressing—
tight
and temporary.

You left
before the war did.
You left
and called it peace.
You left
and the room didn't even notice.

But I did.
I'm still in it.
I never got out.

The call never came.
The call never came.
The call—

Now I have
nothing but time.

And it is
the cruelest weapon.

Time
does not blink.
Time
does not rescue.
Time
does not
call back.

I wasn't your country.
I was just the body
you could bleed
without consequence.

A wound
you refused to dress
because you liked
how I looked
open.

I'm not angry.
I'm holy with it.

I am what happens
when grief gets
a purpose—
and then ripped away.

I am the classified page
you tore out
because it named
what you did to me.

And the craziest part—
I still love you.
You are my all.

I don't blame you.
It's not your fault.

It's mine.

And it is
rancid,
sour,
and sublime.

The decision was mine.
I'll never regret it.

You're the best
worst thing
any harbinger
could bring.

I answered your call.
Carved your name
into my skin,
ink forever, deep.

I became the Manchurian
Candidate,
in your chain of command.

And still—

you
never
picked
up.

Thank you
for giving me
meaning.

I just wish
you could have
told me
how to live
with freedom—

in a broken country
where my brothers
and sisters
don't understand
the cost
we spend
to free them.

If anyone asks
why I scream
in my sleep—

tell them:

**It was never the war.
It was coming home.**

twenty-four
the sum
continuum

These voices—
they are all that's left,
and the only ones I breed.
Because they cannot be seen,
those outside the fight
will never smell the rancid rot
of the disease's might.

I am consumed by my choices—
the death of "me."
It concludes—
only to begin again with the sun's pale climb,
the cyclical demise, relentless, time after time.
Hold on—wait.

Are we our choices, or simply the sum—
of the lessons we've learned
and the places we're from?
The war isn't won, the war never ends—
It lives in my head. It calls itself friend.

I wait.

This is it, an eightfold thread—
the roundabout we can never truly erase.
I love you... not that it ever mattered.
Try to un-live my reality.
I look up, "Hello, how are you?"
I push a smile, "Good, and you?"
It's a prayer.
It's devotion.

And it's mine.

Still I pray,
knee-deep in greed—
a garden of want,
but no soul to feed.
I have too much,
the weight is cracking my chestplate.

Did I make a difference?

Did the water?

I will carry this forever, long after I expire.

My curse: ignite, ignite.

They're gone.
But it's me that's dead.
My war had ended they said,
 not in fire, but kinetic—
I breathe, slow... parasympathetic.

We all do.

Do I?

It all was fated, the way
it ended—
saving you—
something I could
never do.

Obligatory reminders:
the cycle repeats.
The dead rest,
I exist in purgatory,
forever in-between.

But what I mean is—
I am the fire I failed to control.
And the forest
has already named me
god.

It was never the war.
It was coming home.

afterword

I don't know what this anthology looks like to you from the outside. To me, it's a skeleton. A nervous system made visible. I never set out to write poems—I set out to demonstrate what it feels like to exist in a body that was never given peace. Each piece is a synapse misfiring. A memory fragment. A dissociative call into the ether. What you've just read isn't a collection. It's an episode stretched across time. It's the pulse of every moment I didn't know if I would make it. I built this as a system—not as metaphor, but as architecture. The anthology bends, loops, ruptures, and recurs because that's what it's like to live in a brain that has long since stopped trusting its own reflections. It doesn't calm down. It rewires. It short-circuits. It carries its own ghosts like small clots in the bloodstream. I didn't write this so you could understand it. I wrote it so you could feel it. To climb inside the moment before collapse and sit there without resolution—like I do.

If you noticed the structure—how some poems circle, how others detonate, how the anthology starts with a birth and ends in recursion—that wasn't aesthetic. That was anatomy.

Every poem ends with a line that could be the last, because when you live like this, any line might be. The final poem is composed entirely of those lines. Nothing new was written for it. Nothing had to be. That was the moment I realized the anthology was alive. It had already said everything it needed to say. It had bled itself out and then used the blood to sign its name. That final piece isn't a poem. It's aftermath. It's the unhealed scar. The real resonance of every previous scream, reforming into something that finally recognizes itself. That's why it's called *The Sum Continuum*. Because that's what this is —not a beginning, middle, and end. Not a recovery arc. A loop. A system. A soul that never shuts off.

I didn't write this for approval. I didn't write this to be "strong"—it's not. I wrote it because it's real. Some people have experienced this. Some know exactly what this is. For those lucky enough not to know—well, ignorance truly is bliss. Some people actually are able to function, live, breathe, sleep, eat, and even exist without knowing any of this. I wanted to give those lucky individuals a raw look into what the rest of us—the ones written off and forgotten—actually live with. I wrote it to give shape to the part of me I desperately try to suppress just to "live" and function in an arbitrary society. The part that smiles and says, "Good, and you?" while bleeding in twelve invisible directions. The part that can't say what's wrong without sounding like a prayer to the wrong god. The part that knows healing isn't linear—because it isn't healing. It's rebranding pain into something palatable enough to keep breathing.

I know this anthology will be too much for some people. Good. It's too much for me to live. Yet here I am. If you made it to this page, then so are you. I don't care what condition you're in—I care that you're still here. That you kept reading.

That something in you resonated with something in me, even if you don't want to admit it. Maybe especially then. I know this doesn't solve anything. That's the point. I'm not interested in solution. There are none. I'm interested in survival. In witnessing. In tearing open the casing of my life and laying the contents bare—not for closure, but for truth. For whatever's left when language fails and breath remains.

Respectfully, I wasn't writing for critics. I wasn't writing for the literary crowd. I wrote this because it's real. It's my life. It's what keeps me awake. It's why I can't sleep. It's why my nightmares eat my days. This is what trauma feels like. Not metaphor. Not metaphorized. *Felt.* This is what it is to stand on the sidelines of your own life and still call it living. It's rawness. It's implosion. It's beauty, actual pain, and the occasional, impossible flicker of joy. Like life, this anthology is cyclical and woven together. That's not a device—it's anatomy. In *Eightfold Thread*, I used the first lines of the first eight poems. In *The Sum Continuum*, I used the last lines of all twenty-three. That was my nervous system. That was me—head to toe—unstrung and restructured in verse.

So no, this isn't the end. It's just the part where I stop talking and let my words keep speaking for me—keep speaking to you. You're holding what's left of me. That may not mean anything to you. But it will mean everything to the one person who feels the same and is reminded that they're not alone. That is who this anthology is for. You matter. Truth matters. Live life with honesty, compassion, and love. Live every day like it's your last —because nothing is promised or permanent.

Someone once told me, "If you already know it, and can't handle the truth, then don't ask for it."
Reluctantly, I admit—they were right.

This is my truth.
This is my fight.
You're not alone in yours.

True strength is reaching out for help when you need it.